Judith Blacklock's Flower recipes for
SUMMER

The Flower Press

Published by
The Flower Press Ltd
3 East Avenue
Bournemouth
BH3 7BW

Text Copyright © Judith Blacklock, 2008

This first edition published 2008

The moral right of the author has been asserted.

A CIP catalogue record for this book is available from the British Library.

ISBN 13: 978 0 9552391 3 7

Design: Amanda Hawkes

Printed and bound in China by C & C Offset Printing Co., Ltd.

Contents

Introduction

Summer brings an abundance of flowers in the garden and at the florist. There is no limit to what you can do with the wealth of colours, shapes and textures that are available.

I want to encourage you to be inventive with your containers. Cast your eye around your house, garden or even a charity shop or jumble sale and you will begin to see new and interesting containers everywhere. I have given the dimensions of many of the containers used, simply to give an indication of size. You can of course scale up or down according to the plant material you have available and the vase/bowl/dish that you have at home.

Be bold with your choice of colour and texture. Whether you decide to go pale or bright, big or small there are lots of ideas in this book that will get your inspiration going. There are also many fragrant flowers available during the summer season so the design process is even more relaxing and enjoyable.

This book, the third in the series, contains 47 designs that can be made using readily available ingredients. You do not need to be experienced to recreate the arrangements in this book but if you are then use them as a starting point to get creative.

Judith

Perfect pots

Why not recycle glass yoghurt containers to create a set of mini flower vases?

Method

1   First remove the labels from the jars and clean them thoroughly. The best way to do this is to soak them in a sink of warm water for a couple of hours, after which the labels should just slide off.

2   Cut your flowers short and place one stem in each vase.

Design tips

If you are left with a sticky residue on your jars when taking off the labels, nail polish remover should make it disappear completely.

The more vases you have the more you can experiment with pattern and colour. Try arranging them in a heart shape or combining them with tea lights for a dinner party.

Loop the loop

You will need

- container – mine is around 15 cm (6 in) in height
- floral foam
- frog and fix
- 3-5 small hydrangeas
- 3-5 peonies with their foliage
- 5-7 roses
- 5-7 heads of sea holly (*Eryngium*) or teasels (*Dipsacus fullonum*)
- flexi grass
- medium gauge wire

Design tip

Hydrangeas do not generally like being in foam so keep the arrangement topped up and spray the heads regularly with water. In late summer they are much hardier and will last longer without drooping.

The flexi grass loops transform this design of cool colours from the classic to the contemporary.

Method

1 Secure the soaked foam in the container using the frog and fix at the base (Techniques page 94).

2 Insert the flowers and foliage into the foam so that they appear to radiate from a central point until no foam is showing and you have created a rounded, smooth design.

3 Take a few strands of flexi grass and wire them together at each end to give support (Techniques page 97). Insert the wire into the foam to create rhythmic loops around the design.

Pink and gold

This shocking pink container can take equally bright flowers to make a bold statement.

You will need

· pink Perspex® cube vase – this one is 12.5 cm (5 in) square
· gold decorative wire
· sticky tape
· 1 large pink *Hydrangea*
· 3-5 small sunflowers (*Helianthus*)
· 7-9 billy buttons (*Craspedia*)

Design tip

Coloured Perspex® vases are becoming widely available at floristry wholesalers, in a variety of colours and sizes. They do not break as easily as their glass counterparts but they can be scratched by abrasive cleaning and do not look pristine indefinitely.

Method

1 Wrap the decorative wire around the cube vase so that a grid is created over the opening. Use short lengths of sticky tape to secure the wire to the base, to stop it slipping.

2 Add a little water and arrange the flowers in the vase, using the network of wire over the opening to support the stems.

Victoriana

You will need

- smooth sided container, ideally in a colour to harmonize with the flowers – this one is 20cm (8 in) tall
- 3 bunches of sweet William (*Dianthus barbatus*)
- 5-9 stems kentia palm (*Howea forsteriana*)

Design tip

The fronds of the palm will last much longer and give a stronger edge to the design than the leaves of the *Dianthus*.

Long lasting, inexpensive, rich and velvety, the lowly sweet William (*Dianthus barbatus*) was a much favoured flower in Victorian times. This design shows how a traditional flower can be arranged in a subtly contemporary fashion without losing any of its charm.

Method

1 Remove most of the leaves from each stem of the sweet William.

2 Create the right proportions by cutting and placing the sweet Williams in the water-filled container so that the volume of flowers to container is approximately the same.

3 Take the lower leaves off each of the palm stems to give a longer stem. Tuck these around the sweet William to create a frill and to hide the rim of the container.

Pink and lime

You will need

- black cube vase in any material – this one is glass, and 7.5 cm (3 in) square.
- floral foam
- 1 large bright pink peony (*Paeonia*)
- few stems of *Alchemilla mollis*

Design tips

A row of these would look spectacular down the centre of a table, with candles inbetween.

If your peony is small you could add a second to create a larger mass.

Anyone can create this simple design and with just one peony it is an economical way to make a big impression.

Method

1 Place a small amount of soaked foam centrally in the container. Add water.

2 Cut the peony short and place in the foam so the head emerges just above the rim. If the peony is large it may support itself without the foam.

3 Mass *Alchemilla mollis* sprigs around the peony so that their stem ends are in water.

Floating petals

You will need

- low bowl, ideally with an interesting coloured interior – this one is 30 cm (12 in) in diameter
- 1 *Clematis* flower
- 9-12 heads of *Geranium* 'Johnson's Blue'

Design tip

Even when the petals disengage with the flowers they will create wonderful patterns in the water and will last for days.

This design uses *Geranium* 'Johnson's Blue' – a prolific grower in the garden. It is extremely good natured when allowed to float in water. The slightly smaller pink cranesbill (*Geranium sylvaticum*) would work equally well.

Method

1 Pour water into the bowl.

2 Cut the *Clematis* stem short so that it just touches the bottom of the container. Place at the centre.

3 Cut the *Geranium* heads very short and float them around the *Clematis* head.

Rose bowl

Design tips

When using roses from the garden it is rare that one bush will yield enough blooms to create a massed design. This design uses blooms from a selection of bushes.

Using a single type of flower in any design is far easier than trying to combine different types.

Allow a few leaves to remain on the stems to give a natural contrast to the gorgeous blooms of the roses.

Many households still have a rose bowl like this one to display roses from the garden. They are now a valued item hidden in attics, or a must-have at the charity shop or jumble sale. The container has a metal lid with holes through which you can insert the stems.

Method

1 Fill the bowl with water and secure the lid.

2 Cut your roses short and remove any leaves that would be below the water level. If the thorns are long and sharp, cut off the points cleanly with a pair of scissors taking care not to damage the stems. Insert the roses through the holes so that they form a softly domed mass. Do not be fooled, there is quite an art to this!

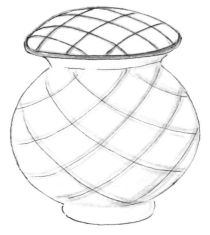

Marguerite

You will need

- small container – this one is 7 x 7 cm (3 x 3 in) in diameter and height
- piece of soaked foam
- 2 stems marguerites (*Argyranthemum frutescens*) or white single spray *Chrysanthemum*
- 1 length of trailing ivy (*Hedera*)

Design tips

Soak the ivy trail under water for 30 minutes before using and it will last longer.

The ox-eye daisy (*Leucanthemum vulgare*) that grows prolifically on the road verge during the summer months is also ideal for this design.

Quick, simple and delightful and all you need is two stems of flowers and a trail of ivy.

Method

1 Place the foam so that it fits the container and rises above the rim but leave a small gap for adding water.

2 Cut the secondary stems off the main stem of the marguerite or spray *Chrysanthemum*. Create the height by placing the first stem centrally.

3 Create a ring of flowers, angling the stems downwards so the head of the flowers extend just over the rim of the container. Your aim is create a ratio of flowers to container of 1.5 : 1 (Techniques page 92).

4 Fill in the space inbetween with other flowers.

5 Tuck the stem end of ivy in the foam, wrap around the top of the container and tuck the tip end into the foam. Cutting the end of the tip and removing the top leaves makes insertion easier.

Summer warmth

You will need

· **glass tank – this one is 10 cm (4 in) square**
· **skein of wool**
· **tumbler, just lower than the height of the tank**
· **3-5 bunches of cornflowers (Centaurea)**

Design tip

Marry your flowers to the colour of your chosen skein – yellow with sunflowers, orange with marigolds or try blue hydrangeas with the blue wool as shown on the right of the page.

This beautiful skein of wool accentuates the blue and purple hues of these gorgeous cornflowers (*Centaurea*). The softness of the wool perfectly complements the frilly petals of the flowers.

Method

1 Arrange the wool in the container so that it covers the sides.

2 Part the wool and place the tumbler into the centre. Carefully add water to the tumbler.

3 Remove all the foliage from the stems and arrange the cornflowers in the tumbler so that they flow over the rim of the container.

Take three

Valerian is a vigorous grower in the summer time, especially in coastal regions. *Alchemilla mollis* and *Geranium* 'Johnson's Blue' are also unafraid to spread. The grouping of these three will provide a stimulating arrangement that will provide colour for weeks throughout the summer.

You will need

· **3 containers of different sizes**
· **3 bunches of different summer flowers. I have used red valerian (*Centranthus ruber*), cranesbill (*Geranium*) and lady's mantle (*Alchemilla mollis*).**

Design tips

At first it was hard to think of colours that would link well with the strong coral red of the valerian but lime green and blue seem to go with just about every colour and this was no exception.

If you use three containers without a common theme, such as glass, it is best to keep it simple and not to use a mixture of flowers within one container.

Method

1   Remove all the foliage that will go below the water level.

2   Place the valerian in the largest container so that the volume of flowers to container is about 1.5:1 (Techniques page 92).

3   Place your flowers in the other containers and group in front of the valerian to make a pleasing composition.

Rock garden

You will need

- tin container – this one is 10 cm (4 in) tall and has an opening 12.5 cm (5 in) square
- pieces of slate in various sizes
- 5-7 cranesbill (*Geranium*)

Design tips

If you have access to large amounts of slate such as broken roof tiles then consider trying this design on a larger scale.

Some tin containers are not waterproof. If in doubt, first line with plastic or place a waterproof container inside.

You could use ferns or succulents as interesting alternatives to the flowers shown.

Broken pieces of slate can often be found in places such as Cumbria. North Wales and Cornwall in the British Isles. The dark grey of the slate gives the impression of rocks or mountains when combined with the seemingly delicate cranesbill (*Geranium*) that thrives in the rock garden.

Method

1 Pack the pieces of slate into the container so that the tallest are at the back and the shortest at the front.

2 Add a little water.

3 Insert the stems of the cranesbills between the pieces of slate so that their ends are in water.

You will need

- piece of plumbers' lead
- scissors
- small plastic container (I used an empty cocktail-stick case)
- an assortment of flowers from the rock garden including thrift (*Armeria maritima*) and rock roses

Design tips

Keep the flowers in scale and in harmony.

Lead is poisonous so take care and wash your hands after use. It can be purchased from the local builders' merchant or DIY store but a friendly plumber can often help out.

Lead the way

Flowers from the rock garden can be grown in the smallest of spaces. This mix of easy-to-grow summer flowers is complemented by the soft grey of a bespoke lead container.

Method

1 Cut the lead with scissors to the size required.

2 Fill a small plastic container with water and wrap the lead firmly around so that it is gripped securely.

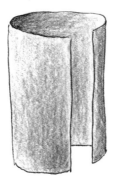

3 Arrange your flowers so that the stem ends are in water.

Pink petals

Add interest to a simple vase arrangement by being inventive with space. Here a single peony bloom takes the colour of the arrangement from bottom to top.

You will need

· glass vase – this one is 20 cm (8 in) tall
· round clear container that sits inside the rim of the vase
· floral foam
· *Aspidistra* leaf
· 8-10 peonies (*Paeonia*) in a variety of colours
· *Alchemilla mollis*

Design tips

The peony at the bottom of the vase is essentially in a greenhouse so will last well in its own mini ecosystem.

To stop the inner container moving use a small amout of fix (see Glossary) to secure the two glass containers together.

Method

1 Place a single peony head in the bottom of the vase with a little water.

2 Secure the round container on top of the vase.

3 Wrap the *Aspidistra* leaf inside around the soaked foam and place the wrapped foam inside the round container. The foam should rise above the rim by about 2.5 cm (1 in).

4 Arrange the peonies into the foam so that they are balanced and evenly spaced.

5 Add the *Alchemilla mollis* to fill any gaps.

You will need

- rectangular straight-sided container – this one is 15 cm (6 in) tall
- black plastic binliner
- soaked floral foam
- sprigs of *Pittosporum variegatum*
- 8-10 white roses
- 7-9 white *Phlox*

Design tip

An approximate guide as to how high foam should rise above the container, in this style of arrangement, is to measure the height of the container and insert foam so that it is 20–25 percent of this height above the rim.

Garden party

The fast growing *Pittosporum* is an ideal candidate for the flower arranger's garden – it is delicate, pretty, tough and needs constant pruning. Here it is combined with a few garden *Phlox* and some roses from the florist.

Method

1 Line the metal container with the binliner as metal containers often leak.

2 Place soaked foam in the container so that it rises above the rim.

3 Create an outline with the *Pittosporum* stems radiating from the centre of the foam to create a strong structure, hiding most of the foam. Angle stems down over the rim.

4 Add roses at regular intervals.

5 Cut the *Phlox* and scatter throughout the arrangement.

Rose tower

You will need

- cylinder vase - this one is 40 cm (15 in) tall and 15 cm (6 in) wide
- pinholder
- glass marbles or pebbles
- 3 roses

Design tips

Try this design with coloured or carbonated water for a different look. Do not try lemonade as the sugar is a food for bacteria.

If you are using a softer stemmed flower in place of the roses, such as tulips, you may need to impale these on the pinholder before adding the marbles or pebbles.

Roses last well under water and this is an unusual way to make three roses go a lot further!

Method

1   Place the pin holder in the bottom of the vase.

2   Pour the glass chips on top of the pinholder. Make sure that they are completely free of dust and dirt.

3   Cut the three roses to graduating lengths and push them firmly onto the pinholder.

4   Fill the container with water.

Lollipop

Giant onions (*Allium*) do not have to be tall and imposing. This design is playful, colourful and simple to create.

Method

1 Soak the foam and cut it to size so that it fits snugly in the container.

2 Cut the *Allium* short and insert it into the centre of the foam.

3 Add the carnations around the base of the *Allium*. Insert one pearl headed pin into the centre of each head.

You will need

- cube vase – this one is 10 cm (4 in) square
- Oasis® Rainbow® floral foam
- 1 giant *Allium*
- 4/5 green carnations (*Dianthus*) such as *D.* 'Prado'
- purple, pearl headed pins (optional)

Design tips

The important thing to consider when creating a design such as this is that the head of the main flower should be of roughly the same volume as the container.

If you do not have coloured foam then wrap an *Aspidistra* leaf around green foam. See the design on pages 34–35.

31

Pair of peonies

You will need

- letterbox shaped container – this one is 14 cm (5½ in) high 29 cm (11 in) wide 7 cm (2½ in) deep
- 2 white peonies (*Paeonia*) with their foliage
- short sprays of *Euonymus* or other cream variegated foliage
- 2-3 stems of China grass (*Liriope muscari*)
- florists' fix

Design tips

Peonies are deciduous but the foliage grows early and stays on the plant until the frosts arrive. It is a versatile, strong foliage with lovely colours later in the year.

China grass acts well out of water. You could alternatively use lily grass (*Liriope gigantea*) or a strip of variegated *Phormium* leaf avoiding the stiff central rib.

A letterbox shaped vase is great for when you only have a few flowers to display. This black container has been embellished with a few strands of China grass to add a little style.

Method

1 Remove all the foliage from your peonies and use it to fill the container, with a few of the leaves angled over the rim.

2 Cut the peonies short and place them in the centre.

3 Place the *Euonymus* judiciously through the design.

4 Place a small blob of fix on each side of the container. Wrap the China grass around the container and over the fix so that it stays in place.

Cool colours

You will need

- **cube vase – this one is 12 cm (5 in) square**
- **soaked foam**
- **3-5 *Aspidistra* leaves**
- **pin**
- **salal tips (*Gaultheria*)**
- **7 yellow roses**
- **1 blue *Hydrangea***
- **5-7 stems of bear grass or flexi grass**
- **1 stem of *Hypericum***

Design tip

**You could also try threading holly berries, cranberries or small *Chrysanthemum* heads onto the flexi grass.
If you find it difficult to push the grass through, first make a hole with strong wire, a sewing needle or a cocktail stick.**

This is a design for a hot day – the use of lemon yellow and pale blue give the design a refreshing sense of calm.

Method

1   Cut a piece of soaked foam to fit inside the cube with about 1.25 cm (½ in) to spare on each side. It should be approximately the same height as the container.

2   Wrap an *Aspidistra* leaf tightly around the foam and secure with a pin. Place into the cube.

3   Create a covering of foliage over the foam, grouping the plant material. Fold the *Aspidistra* leaves (Techniques page 97). Place the salal tips on one side and the folded *Aspidistra* leaves on the other.

4   Insert the stem of *Hydrangea* centrally. Group the roses at the front and the rest behind.

5   Remove the berries from the *Hypericum* stem. Thread a few berries onto each stem of flexi or bear grass with intervals between. Leave the two ends free for insertion into the foam.

6   Loop the berried grass over the design to create enclosed space.

Elderflower cordial

You will need

- shallow bowl or deep plate – this shallow bowl is 23 cm (9 in) in diameter
- deeper, smaller bowl
- 3-4 heads elderflower
- 1 head of *Petunia* or any other round flower such as a mini *Gerbera*

Design tip

The outer bowl is not essential but it will catch the tiny flowers of the elderflowers as they drop and saves on housekeeping.

The common elder (*Sambucus nigra*) grows prolifically in every British hedgerow during the summer months. Its creamy flat heads are held on woody stems and can look inelegant as a cut flower in a vase. Cutting the heads short and placing them in a low bowl they create a mass of starry flowers and also provide a support for other flowers, such as a single *Petunia*.

Method

1 Fill the bowl with water. Place on the lower bowl or dish.

2 Cut the stems of the elderflower short and float them in the water.

3 Cut the *Petunia* and thread the stem through the elderflowers.

Box of blooms

You will need

- **cardboard box – this one is 15 cm (6 in) in height**
- **glass tumbler of a height to rise approximately two-thirds of the way up the box**
- **sweet peas (*Lathyrus*) in a mix of colours**
- ***Alchemilla mollis***

Design tip

You can buy gift boxes with fabulous colours and patterns from most gift shops. Do not discard the lids – line them with a little plastic and a thin slab of foam and create a tapestry design (see page 86) from your leftover flowers and foliage.

The one thing everyone has lying around the house is some sort of cardboard box just too good to throw away. If it is an interesting colour or texture, why not use it to display some flowers?

Method

1   Place the tumbler inside the box. Make sure it will not tip – if the box has an uneven base then you could use a little fix to keep the glass in place.

2   Add the sweet peas to create a gently rounded outline, and then thread the *Alchemilla* through the design.

Perfect pink

The strength of this design lies in the use of colour. The inspiration came from finding a bowl that was the perfect match for the fluffy pink *Begonia*.

You will need

- low coloured bowl – this one is 17 cm (7 in) in diameter
- small round leaves. I used the fleshy, long lasting leaves of London pride (*Saxifraga*)
- 1 head of double *Begonia*

Method

1 Fill the bowl with water.

2 Arrange the leaves in a circle around the bowl.

3 Cut the *Begonia* short and place centrally.

Design tip

Begonias are ideal for patio pots and window boxes. They are easy-going and flower prolifically over the summer months. The double flowers are particularly attractive and come in an array of colours which can be matched to the bowl of your choice.

Summer sushi

You will need

- **flat dish or tray** – this one is 21 cm (8½ in) square
- **floral foam**
- *Aspidistra* **leaves**
- **pearl headed pins**
- *Hypericum* **berries**
- **carnations in a mix of colours**

Design tip

If you wish to place the designs directly on to a table or other surface, pin a small square of plastic bag to the base using mossing pins before you wrap the foam with the leaf.

These stylish wraps of *Aspidistra*, *Hypericum* and carnation (*Dianthus*) are a quick and inexpensive way to decorate a table or create an individual place setting.

Method

1 Cut the foam into blocks roughly 3 x 3 x 10 cm (1 x 1 x 4 in).

2 Cut off the stem and stiff part of each *Aspidistra* leaf. Wrap each block of foam in a leaf with the flatter side of the leaf along the bottom. Secure with a pin and cut off any excess at the top of the foam.

3 Cut the carnations short and insert one into the top of each wrapped parcel. Tuck short sprigs of *Hypericum* around the flower heads.

4 Arrange your 'sushi' on a tray and add some water to keep the foam wet.

Elastic

You will need

· **glass container – this one is 15 cm (6 in) in height and width and 7.5 cm (3 in) deep**
· **about 12 rubber bands of a uniform size and colour**
· **one flower of choice**

Design tip

Try tucking autumnal leaves between the container and the bands, or stems of lavender (*Lavandula*) which will dry in situ and give a different finish.

A rubber band is one of those dispensable articles that we never have when needed. Collect the bands the postman leaves behind to make a mechanic that gives a completely new look to a standard glass container.

Method

1 Ensure the bands are of a size that will fit snugly around your container.

2 Place these at regular intervals around your container, both horizontally and vertically.

3 Fill the container with water.

4 Cut your flower and insert through one of the holes in the network of bands so that the stem end is in water.

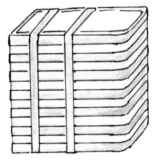

Subtle stems

You will need

- **fishbowl vase – this one is 30 cm (12 in) at its widest point**
- **5-7 calla lilies (*Zantedeschia*)**
- **gold aluminium wire**

Design tips

If callas are left out of water for a couple of hours the stems become limp and are easier to manipulate into curves.

The water will need to be changed daily and the stem ends trimmed to minimize the spread of bacteria to which callas are particularly susceptible.

This rhythmic design uses just a few stems to great effect.

Method

1   Callas often come with very long stems so you may need to cut them down. Keep the cut off stems. Place a couple of the cut off stems into the vase so that they form additional curves.

2   Add water to the bowl. Curve the flowers into the bowl so that they fill the space effectively and have their stem ends in water.

3   Push short lengths of slightly twisted aluminium wire into some of the stems to join them together.

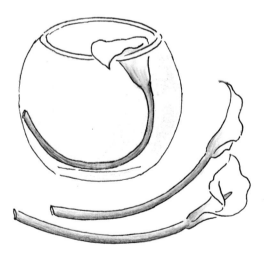

Beading

An empty glass yoghurt pot provides the perfect container for two blooms of *Cymbidium* orchid.

You will need

- glass yoghurt pot, jar or tumbler
- beads
- 2 heads of *Cymbidium* orchid

Design tips

You could make many of these arrangements and place them in a line down the centre of the table or on a low window ledge. Try and link the colour of your flowers with the beads. Here the pink on the throat of the flowers picks up the colour of the beads.

Old strings of beads are readily available from charity shops and jumble sales.

Method

1 Fill the container with beads.

2 Add water.

3 Insert the stems of the two orchids through the beads into the water.

Fragrant lavender

You will need

· ceramic cube container
· thick decorative aluminium wire
· thin decorative wire
· 2 bunches of fresh lavender (*Lavandula*)
· 7-10 individual *Hydrangea* florets (1 head)

Design tips

If you want to try this design using flowers that do not dry as well as the lavender, place the container on a flat dish with a little water so that the stems outside the container are in water.

Pick lavender for drying when there is an even mix of flowers and buds on the stem.

Both lavender and hydrangeas dry beautifully and so can survive out of water in late summer when mature. This design can be created using lavender from the garden and will last and last.

Method

1 Start by creating two wire structures – one to support the stems within the container and the second to lie across the container's opening. Wrap the thick aluminium wire around a marker pen to create a flat mass of loops for the top and a smaller mass to fit inside.

2 Using the thin decorative wire, bind the lavender into small bunches. Cut the stem ends neatly to a uniform length. Thread the bunches through the loops in and around the container.

3 Place the *Hydrangea* florets through the design.

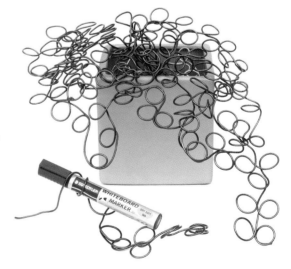

51

Water lilies

You will need

- salad bowl
- large plain green ivy leaves
- 3 *Chrysanthemum* – bloom type with a large single head rather than a spray form

Design tips

You could use mini *Gerbera*, *Gerbera* or even water lilies themselves to create a long lasting effective design. Here the colour of the flowers links with the inside colour of the bowl.

If you wish you could make a neat, clean incision with a knife through the centre of the leaves and insert the flower stems through.

A few large ivy leaves, three bloom chrysanthemums and a coloured salad bowl is all you need to create this quick and easy design.

Method

1 Fill the bowl two thirds with water.

2 Wash the ivy leaves in water to which a drop of liquid soap has been added to ensure they are clean. Place on the surface of the bowl.

3 Cut the *Chrysanthemum* blooms short and float on the water.

Stripes

A great way to use up leftover flowers and play with colour combinations, this design could not be simpler.

You will need

- rectangular container – this one is 5 cm (2 in) deep
- floral foam
- pieces of broken slate. These are old roof slates.
- flowers in a combination of colours and textures such as carnations (*Dianthus*), pincushion protea (*Leucospermum*), gentian (*Gentiana*) and globe thistle (*Echinops*) used here.

Design tips

You could use a low open casserole dish for this design if you cannot find a rectangular container. Flat mother-of-pearl shells can be used instead of the slate, but make sure you link the colours accordingly.

Method

1 Cut a slice from a block of foam about 2.5 cm (1 in) thick and cover the base of the container.

2 Place the slate pieces into the foam diagonally, across the container, so that you have space between to add the stripes of flowers.

3 Cut the flowers short and add them to the design in stripes, making sure that adjacent stripes combine colours and textures effectively.

You will need

- cylindrical Perspex® container – this one is 15 cm (6 in) both in height and width
- 7-10 orange roses
- 4-6 orange spray roses
- 4-6 *Euphorbia*
- garden twine
- coil of decorative wire in a coordinating colour

Design tips

When creating the spiral you may find your flowers form a fan shape which is difficult to hold. If so, relax your hand and the stems will create a more circular form.

Take care when handling *Euphorbia* that you wash your hands well afterwards since the milky latex contained in the stem is poisonous.

Hotwire

A monochromatic handtied bouquet looks great displayed in a coordinating container. The addition of a coil of decorative wire gives a little bit of glitz.

Method

1   Cut a length of string about 1 m (40 in) long and drape it around your neck so it does not get lost.

2   Prepare your stems by removing the foliage and thorns so that only the top pair of leaves remain.

3   To make the handtied, place your first stem in your hand and steady it with your thumb. Place the second stem diagonally over the first, with the head pointing towards the shoulder of the hand you are using.

4   Continue in this way until your stems form a spiral in your hand. If you need to create better balance cross a stem behind in the opposite direction. Tie the bunch securely with the twine.

5   Squeeze the stems together and cut them so that they are a uniform length. Pour water into the container. Slip the coil of wire into the water and add your handtied bouquet.

You will need

- **watermelon**
- **sharp pointed knife**
- **tooth/cocktail picks**
- **kebab sticks**
- ***Hypericum* berries**
- ***Skimmia* or other firm berries**
- **crab apples**

Design tip

This design will keep for several days if kept in a plastic bag in the vegetable department of the refrigerator. Blow into the bag to create a mini greenhouse.

You need to use hard fruits and berries that are unblemished so that deterioration is slow.

Watermelon surprise

An original alternative as a table centrepiece this design will be sure to keep your guests smiling.

Method

1 With a sharp knife cut out a section of your watermelon that is approximately one fifth of the whole fruit.

2 Impale each of the *Hypericum* berries on a pick and create a line along the edge of the melon.

3 Create further lines with the other fruits and berries using short tooth/cocktail picks or longer kebab sticks depending on the depth they have to reach into the flesh to be secure.

Strawberries and cream

You will need

- **square container in a pale colour – this one is 9 cm (3½ in) high and 11 cm (4 in) wide**
- **piece of foam to fit the inside of the container and extend half the height above**
- **sisal in a pale colour**
- **mossing pins**
- **cream lisianthus (*Eustoma*)**
- **strawberries**
- **cocktail sticks**
- **flexi grass**

Design tip

The strawberries must be at their firmest for this design or they will simply slide down the cocktail sticks or rapidly go mushy.

Perfect for a summer's day, this design looks good enough to serve at Wimbledon!

Method

1 Create a rounded top to the foam by cutting it above the rim with a knife to make a shape that is roughly domed. With your hands rub the top until it appears spherical.

2 Soak the foam and place it in the container.

3 Cover the foam with a thin layer of sisal and pin in place with the mossing pins.

4 Insert the lisianthus into the foam, being sure to maintain the rounded shape. Use a mixture of the smaller and larger heads and buds.

5 Push a cocktail stick into the bottom of each strawberry, just far enough to create a stalk.

6 Add the strawberries to the design.

7 Add the flexi grass in loops throughout the design to enclose the space.

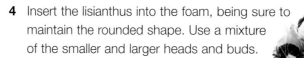

Super *superba*

You will need

- rectangular plastic dish
- floral foam
- florists' tape
- *Eucalyptus cinerea*
- leather leaf (*Arachniodes*)
- Boston Ivy (*Parthenocissus tricuspidata*) or large ivy leaves
- 5-7 *Hypericum* or ivy leaves
- 5 pincushion protea (*Leucospermum*)
- 7-9 *Gloriosa superba* 'Rothschildiana'
- 7 red roses
- 7 yellow roses

Design tip

If you want to be sure of good colour harmony, link the flowers in some way. Here you have red and yellow roses, and the two colours within the *Gloriosa* link the three flowers together.

Gloriosa superba 'Rothschildiana' always looks impressive, with its shocking pink and sunshine yellow petals.

Method

1. Soak the foam and tape the soaked foam to the container. Leave space around the edge for a reservoir of water.

2. Create the outline using the *Eucalyptus*. Each stem should appear to radiate from a central point.

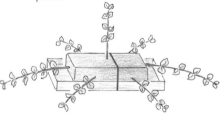

3 Fill in the outline with the *Parthenocissus* and leather leaf. Do not exceed the boundaries that you have created with the *Eucalyptus*.

4 Add the flowers and berries to the arrangement.

Rows of roses

Simple to make, this design could use as many or as few roses as you have available.

You will need

- **rectangular container – this one is 14 cm (5¹/₂ in) high and wide and 10 cm (4 in) deep**
- **floral foam**
- **large *Aspidistra* leaf**
- **mossing pins**
- **flat moss**
- **enough roses to cover the top of the container**
- ***Hypericum* berries**
- **flexi grass**

Design tips

Try recreating this design with a single rose in a tiny square vase – it would make a great place setting.

Moss can be purchased from the florist or taken from the lawn.

Method

1 Measure your container and cut your floral foam so that it is 2.5 cm (1 in) smaller in all dimensions.

2 Wrap the soaked foam in the *Aspidistra* leaf and secure with mossing pins.

3 Place the wrapped foam into the container.

4 Cut your roses short and insert them in neat rows into the foam.

5 Divide the moss into small pieces and push it down the sides of the container to meet the top edge of the *Aspidistra* leaf.

6 Thread the *Hypericum* berries on to short lengths of flexi grass. If you cannot make a hole in the berry with the grass use a pin or cocktail stick.

7 Insert the flexi grass into the foam to make loops over the design.

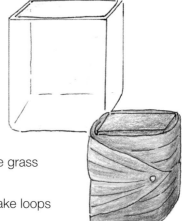

You will need

- small oval or round container – this one is 12.5 cm (5 in) wide and 10 cm (4 in) tall
- floral foam
- 3 pink mini *Gerbera*
- 1 *Celosia argentea* var. *cristata*
- 6-8 crab apples (*Malus*)
- cocktail sticks

Design tips

If you have difficulty inserting the stems in the foam use a heavier stem, such as that of a rose, to make a hole prior to insertion.

Remove a small amount of foam vertically from the back of the foam so that water can be added with a long spouted watering can.

Use quince or mini apples if you do not have crab apples.

Appetising

A tiny design that will brighten up any room but uses only a few flowers.

Method

1   Cut the foam to size and chamfer the edges (Techniques page 94). Wedge the foam into the container and cut the top so it is level with the rim.

2   Insert your flowers and apples in small groups. Save the excess stems of the *Gerbera* to use separately.

3   Push a cocktail stick into the base of each crab apple and add these to the design.

4   Use the cut stems of the mini *Gerbera* to finish the design and to balance the apples on the opposite side.

Coconut cream

You will need

- **round vase – this one is 16 cm (6 in) high**
- **chicken wire**
- **1 large *Hydrangea***
- **3 peonies**
- **5 roses**

Design tip

You could use a real coconut shell to make a smaller version of this design.

This beautiful ceramic container has come to be known as the coconut vase at the flower school, and you can see why!

Method

1 Crumple the chicken wire into the container so that it is just visible above the rim (Techniques page 96).

2 Add the *Hydrangea* first, then the peonies and then the roses. Make sure you have an even balance of colour and that the design is nicely domed.

At the sea shore

The cool colours and textures work perfectly with the clear glass to give the mood of summer days at the seaside.

Method

1 Soak the foam and place in the centre of the cube.

2 Cut the individual heads off the sea holly and divide between the vases keeping them just long enough for the flowers to appear above the rim. Add the *Phlox*.

3 Pour the tiny shells into each vase to rise two thirds up the cubes.

4 Place a large spiral shell on the top of the shells in each container.

You will need

· 3 glass cube vases – these are 8 cm (3 in) square
· 3 cubes floral foam about 2.5 cm (1 in) square
· bag tiny sea shells of a uniform shape
· 1 stem sea holly (*Eryngium*)
· 3 stems *Phlox*
· 3 large spiral shells

Design tip

The tiny shells have lots of subtle colour and patterns to give contrast and interest. Avoid using a mixture of different types of shell as this gives an over busy effect.

Five supermarket roses

You will need

- decorative ovenware such as a low casserole dish – this one is 27 cm (11 in) long and 18 cm (7 in) wide
- small rectangular piece of foam to fill approximately two thirds of the dish lengthways
- 5 roses
- wild fennel (*Foeniculum vulgare*)
- *Hydrangea* leaves
- pins made from bent stub wire

Design tip

In the spring you could use Queen Anne's lace (*Ammi majus*) or cow parsley (*Anthriscus sylvestris*) instead of fennel or you could use rosemary (*Rosmarinus*) or oregano (*Origanum*) as an alternative in the summer.

By mid summer *Hydrangea* leaves are strong and robust and provide a decorative means of hiding foam. The beauty of this design comes from linking the distinctive coral pink colour of the roses with that of the container.

Method

1 Soak the foam and place it lengthwise along the dish.

2 Place the fennel across the foam, staggering the heights.

3 Take the roses and position at different levels within the framework of the fennel.

4 Pour a little water into the dish.

5 Pin the *Hydrangea* leaves against the foam to cover it at the front, back and sides.

Summer meadow

You will need

- **small posy pad – this one is 12 cm (5 in) in diameter**
- **dried or fresh wheat (*Triticum*)**
- **mossing pins or medium gauge wire**
- **raffia**
- **sneezeweed (*Helenium*)**
- **marjoram (*Origanum*)**
- **brodiaea (*Triteleia*)**

Design tips

The wheat will dry in situ and you need only replace the flowers. A few stems of faux flowers such as field poppies and dried lavender would make a lasting design to enjoy throughout the year.

If you cannot find a posy pad then cut a circle of foam and wrap its base in plastic to protect surfaces.

Evocative of walks in the country, this design is simple and sunny.

Method

1   Soak the posy pad and allow any excess water to drip away.

2 Using the mossing pins secure the wheat in small bunches of two or three stems around the circumference of the posy pad. If you do not have mossing pins then bend short lengths of wire into a hairpin shape and use these instead.

3 Wrap the raffia around the base of the design to hide the mechanics.

4 Thread flowers into the arrangement so that they stand upright at the same height as the wheat or slightly taller. Cut a few shorter stems to poke through the wheat.

Terracotta pot

You will need

- **terracotta pot – this one is 20 cm (8 in) tall**
- **terracotta base (optional)**
- **line plant material such as _Frittilaria_, stocks**
- **line foliage such as dogwood (_Cornus_)**
- **round plant material such as roses or open lilies**
- **spray plant material such as _Astilbe_**

Design tip

If you feel your proportions are not perfect, and your container just a little too low, add a base as shown.

The rich abundance of summer is shown in this lavish design using tints, tones and shades of one colour.

Method

1 Line your container if it is not waterproof. Place foam in the container so that it rises above the rim of the container.

2 Create an outline with your foliage (see line drawing opposite).

3 Reinforce the foliage shape created with linear flowers.

4 Add your round flowers. These are the most dominant shaped flowers and will hold your design together.

5 Fill in with your remaining plant material.

Pom-pommes

This bright and unusual colour combination is a cheerful addition to any home.

You will need

- letterbox shaped container – this one is 14 cm (5½ in) high 29 cm (11 in) wide 7 cm (2½ in) deep
- floral foam
- *Galax* or round ivy leaves
- 5-7 carnations (*Dianthus*)
- 4 pom-pom *Chrysanthemum*
- large crab apples (*Malus*) or small apples
- cocktail sticks
- snake grass (*Equisetum hyemale*)

Design tip

Soak *Galax* or ivy leaves under water for 10 minutes. Shake off the excess and place in a sealed plastic bag in the vegetable compartment of your refrigerator. They will last for weeks.

Method

1   Cut the foam to fit the container. Make sure it rises above the rim and leave space at either end for adding water.

2   Add the *Galax* or ivy leaves so that they are angled over the rim of the container. Do not make them too regimented – position them in different directions to create a loose effect.

3   Insert the *Dianthus* into the foam in groups so that each has a round leaf below or behind it.

4   Cut the pom-pom chrysanthemums at varying lengths and add them to the design. At this point my design became asymmetric.

5   Insert a cocktail stick into the base of each apple and add these in a group to one side of the arrangement.

6   Bend the snake grass stems in two places to form a goal shape and insert the ends into the foam to complete the arrangement.

Rusty roses

This elegant design looks far more complicated than it is. All it takes is a little concentration and patience and you can achieve something fabulous.

You will need

- urn shaped container – this one is 25 cm (10 in) tall
- piece of floral foam or a foam sphere to fit the opening
- 15-20 roses

Design tips

It is cheating a bit, but if you are placing the arrangement somewhere with a wall directly behind it then you can save money and time by making the front half only and forgetting the back.

This type of design uses a lot of flowers as no space is involved (and space is cheap!). To make your roses go further use small sprigs of small leaved foliage such as box (*Buxus*), myrtle (*Myrtus*) or ming fern (*Asparagus umbellatus*) between the flowers.

Method

1. Place the soaked sphere into the opening of the container.
2. Start by placing one rose centrally on a short stem.
3. Add the roses around the rim of the container so that they create an even circle. When complete, the width of the design should be approximately equal to the height of the container.
4. Fill in the area in between with the remaining roses. Avoid creating concentric circles as the design will look contrived and you will be more restricted by the number of stems needed.

Ball of blooms

In this design the massed hydrangeas provide the mechanics to keep the other flowers in position. The sweet peas are simply threaded through where they will stay securely in place.

You will need

- spherical container – this one is 15 cm (6 in) high and 20 cm (8 in) wide
- 3-5 hydrangeas
- 20-25 sweet peas (*Lathyrus*)

Design tips

Hydrangeas and sweet peas drink a lot of water so keep the arrangement topped up and spray them from time to time.

Sweet peas are easy to grow and cutting them encourages further blooms to form.

Method

1 Place water in the container and arrange the hydrangeas so that they form a domed mass and hide the rim.

2 Thread the sweet peas inbetween the individual flowers of the hydrangeas so that they are evenly spaced.

Gooseberry fool

You will need

- **round low glass bowl –
  this one is 20 cm (8 in)
  in diameter and 6 cm
  (2½ in) high**
- **1-2 packs of 'Helda'
  beans**
- **1 small carton of
  gooseberries**
- **few heads from a stem
  of *Cymbidium* or
  Dendrobium orchid**
- **cotton wool**
- **thin wool or thread**

Design tip

**Helda beans are more
flexible than runner
beans and can therefore
be more easily
manipulated around
corners and curves.**

The smooth ridged form of the beans is
complemented by the hairy round gooseberries to
create a fun floral design for an outside barbecue.

Method

1   Arrange the beans around the inside of the container, working inwards
    from the edge. Make sure that the ends are staggered.

2   Fill the centre with the gooseberries
    allowing a few to spill over
    the beans.

3   Remove the individual
    heads from the orchid.
    Soak a small amount
    of cotton wool in
    water and wrap it
    around the bottom
    of each stem. Secure
    with the thread or wool.

4   Place the orchid stems
    between the gooseberries.

Bubblegum

The plastic ice-cube bubbles in this simple design keep the stems in place and add texture to this shocking pink container.

You will need

- brightly coloured cube container – mine is Perspex®
- re-freezable ice-cube bubbles (available from many homeware shops)
- roses or other round headed flower in a colour to match the container

Design tip

With a little effort it is possible to stack the bubbles into neat rows for a more uniform effect.

Method

1 Place your ice bubbles within the container and fill with water.

2 Remove the leaves from the roses as they will be too far down the stem to be seen.

3 Cut the stems short so that they are supported by the bubbles and their heads rest just above the rim of the container.

4 Frame the roses by tucking the separated rose leaves underneath.

Tapestry of flowers

You will need

- low bowl – this one is 30 cm (12 in) in diameter and 8 cm (3 in) deep
- small piece of foam
- 2 gentian (*Gentiana*)
- 3-5 pink roses
- 3-2 globe thistle (*Echinops*)
- 3-5 mini *Gerbera*
- 3-5 red roses
- foliage such as moss, *Galax*, Boston ivy (*Parthenocissus tricuspidata*), ming fern (*Asparagus umbellatus*) and rosemary (*Rosmarinus*)
- apples (*Malus*)

Design tip

When planning the placement of the flowers and foliage be sure that the more intricately formed plant material is positioned next to those with a plainer texture or form to show each off to greater advantage.

Rich jewel colours create a stunning tapestry of flowers, ideal for placing on a low table. If you have a lovely mix of different textures and forms you will only need a few flowers for this design. However, if you have the flowers available it is great fun to create wonderful patterns with colour and form.

Method

1   Cut the soaked foam so that it rises to just below the rim of the container and fills one third to one half of the bowl.

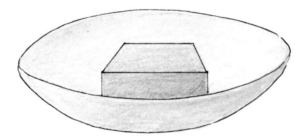

86

2　Cover the majority of the foam with foliage, used in groups to create contrast of texture and form.

3　Add the flowers, again in groups to create a tapestry of colour, form and texture. There should be little or no space between the elements.

Design tip

The majority of the foliage in this design should be plain green. Too much variegated foliage creates an over busy effect.

Think pink

You will need

- **container with a country feel – this one is 17 cm (7 in) square**
- **floral foam**
- **hard ruscus (*Ruscus hypoglossum*)**
- **stocks (*Matthiola*)**
- **salal (*Gaultheria*)**
- **honeysuckle (*Lonicera*)**
- ***Lysimachia***
- **peonies (*Paeonia*)**

Design tips

It is rarely possible to buy honeysuckle from the florist but if you do not have it growing in the garden you may find it in the hedgerows or hanging over a neighbour's wall.

Baskets have a natural affinity with summer flowers but check that yours is waterproof before you add foam or water.

Sometimes there is nothing better than pink, pink and more pink – especially in the summer when there is so much around.

Method

1 Make sure the container is waterproof. Secure the soaked foam inside it.

2 Create a strong outline using the hard ruscus reinforced with the salal (*Gaultheria*) (Techniques page 95).

3 Add your other flowers, maintaining the outline that you have made.

Plastic fantastic

You will need

- glass vase, wider at the base than at the top – this one is 20 cm (8 in) high
- black plastic tubing for tidying wires, approximately 2.5 cm (1 in) diameter.
- 1 stem *Cymbidium* orchid
- 1 large *Anthurium*
- 5-7 *Aspidistra* leaves
- 3-5 *Fatsia* leaves
- bear grass (*Xerophyllum*)
- salal (*Gaultheria*)
- florists' tape

Design tip

If the *Aspidistra* leaves try to escape your hand, you can use florist fix on the tips to secure against the stems.

This design uses plastic tubing usually used to tidy up a mess of wires as an innovative addition to a glass vase.

Method

1. Coil the plastic tubing around the inside of the vase and tuck the end in so that it does not uncoil. Add water.

2. Create an arrangement of flowers in the hand. Hold the long stem of *Cymbidium* orchid in the left had (if you are right handed) and add the *Fatsia* and *Anthurium* at the base of the lowest orchid head.

3. Add the *Aspidistra* leaves to the bunch, pulling the tips down into your hand together with the stem ends to create loops.

4. Use the salal to add volume at the bottom of the design if needed.

5. Create space with loops of bear grass.

6. Bind the flowers together in a bunch with florists' tape to secure them and cut the stems so that they are level.

7. Place the arrangement in the vase, making sure that the foliage rests around the rim.

Techniques

Conditioning

- As soon as stems are removed from their supply of water the end seals and will no longer take up water unless the stem is re-cut. Cut the stems at an angle to provide a larger surface area for the uptake of water.
- Remove all foliage that falls below the waterline. Once submerged leaves deteriorate rapidly so causing bacteria to multiply.

General guidelines for arranging

Balance

Most of the designs in this book use symmetrical balance, i.e. if an imaginary line is drawn down the centre the visual weight each side will appear equal. It is vital that your work does not fall over and does not appear to want to fall over so ensure it is balanced top to bottom, side to side and front to back.

Scale

It is vital that your flowers are in scale with one another to achieve a harmonious design. This means that no flower should be more than twice as large as the one next to it in size. For example, a sunflower (*Helianthus*) and a *Craspedia* are not in scale with one another as the former is about 10 times the size of the latter. However, if the smaller flowers are massed in small groups then the scale will work.

Form

As a general guide most flowers can be classified as being round (such as a *Gerbera*, peony, sunflower, *Dahlia*), spray (such as *Limonium*, *Gypsophila*, *Hypericum*, spray carnation) or linear (*Delphinium*, gladioli, lavender). Round flowers are the key players. They are the most dominant form in design and should be included in all work using mixed flowers (see pages 29, 63). Spray flowers are the supporting actors and give softness and interest to the design (see page 27). Linear flowers are important in contemporary and large scale work and parallel design (see page 91 for use in contemporary work).

Proportion

This is important to consider when doing vase work, where the volume of plant material to volume of container is 1.5:1 or 1:1.5 if the container is of special interest and the most important part of the design.

Alternatively the ratio of the *height* of the plant material to that of the container should be 1.5:1 if only a few vertical flowers are used. If the container is wire then the height of the plant material to the width of the container should be 1:1.5.

Floral foam

Using floral foam

A water absorbing material which supports stems at virtually any angle. OASIS® is a well-known brand name. Floral foam is most commonly available in a brick-sized block but is also available in cones, cylinders, rings, spheres and a myriad of other shapes. There is also a coloured foam called OASIS® Rainbow® Foam. This takes much longer to soak and you will need to add cut flower food.

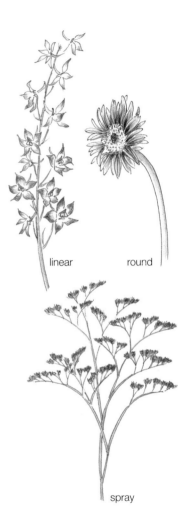

linear   round

spray

Preparing foam

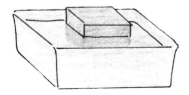

Measure the size of the piece of foam required and cut it carefully. Place the foam horizontally onto water that is deeper than the piece of foam you wish to soak. Allow the foam to sink under its own weight until the top if level with the water and the colour has changed from light to dark green. Always keep a reservoir of water in the bottom of your container from which the foam can draw.

Securing foam in a container

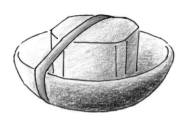

To secure foam in a container you can either:

- Place florists' fix on the base of a four pronged disc called a 'frog'.
- Place this on the clean, dry surface of your container and impale your soaked foam on the frog.

or

- Use florists' tape across the top of your foam and down the two sides of the container.

Storing foam

Once foam has been soaked store it in a tied plastic bag. In this way the foam will remain wet and keep for ages. If soaked foam is left in the open air it will dry out and will not take up further supplies of water.

Chamfering foam

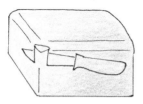

This means removing all the sharp edges to achieve a smoother and more rounded overall shape. It can also allow room for adding water to a finished design.

Making a foliage outline

The designs on pages 62 and 74 are based on a strong foundation of foliage. In order to do this effectively it is recommended that:

- the foam rises higher than the container so that stems can be easily angled down over the rim of the container. Then the container and arrangement appear as one, rather than as two separate parts.
- the foliage should appear to radiate from the centre of the foam. In a design where the overall appearance is round, the foliage will radiate like the spokes of a wheel if seen from above (see illustration right).
- a strong three dimensional form is created by radiating stems from the top of the foam as well as the sides.

Alternative stem supports

Pinholders

Pinholders, or kenzans as they are known in Japan, are stem supports (otherwise known as a mechanic). They are ideal for:

- soft stems that are difficult to insert in foam such as anemones
- woody stems that are often too heavy to stay happily in place in floral foam, such as lilac (*Syringa*) and guelder rose (*Viburnum opulus* 'Roseum')

A pinholder consists of a multitude of short metal pins in a heavy base which is usually, but not always, round. They may be purchased in a wide variety of sizes from the minute 1.5 cm (½ in) to the large 15 cm (6 in). The most easily found is 6.5 cm (2½ in). To secure, place a coil of florists' fix on the base of the pinholder and position it firmly on a clean dry base.

Flowers with soft stems can be simply cut and impaled on the pinholder. Woody stems need to be cut at an angle and, if you wish, make a short slit up from the base.

Adhesive tape

Transparent adhesive tape can be used to create a grid over the opening of glass containers to give support. You can use tape available from stationers; it will work well as long as it is suitably narrow and the vase is dry. There is also a specialist clear tape available that will adhere to wet surfaces and may be worth buying if you often work with glass.

Tubes

Glass test tubes are a useful way to use flowers in more structural and unusual designs and still give them the water that they need. You can also obtain plastic tubes with lids through which a stem can be inserted – these are often used for orchids. These are less attractive but there are various methods of disguising them (such as wrapping them with small leaves or moss). They are available in a variety of sizes. They also have the advantage that they can be secured at any angle and will not spill their contents. Some glass tubes are now manufactured with holes at the rim for hanging.

Chicken wire (wire netting)

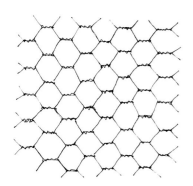

Sometimes known as wire netting, this can be used inside a container and is the ideal method of securing soft stems and flowers which need a lot of water such as spring flowers.

The ideal mesh size for this purpose is the 5 cm (2 in). The amount you use depends to some extent on the size of the container and the thickness of the stems you wish to insert. A rough guideline would be to cut a piece a little wider than the width of the opening and three times the depth. Cut off the selvedge as this is stiff. Crumple the netting so that it forms approximately the same shape as the container.

Fill the container with water and thread your stems through the chicken wire. If the mesh of your wire is small the holes will disappear to nothing once you have several layers.

If you need extra support, particularly if you are using thick stemmed heavy branches, place a pinholder in the bottom of your container. Allow your first placement through the chicken wire to be well impaled on the pinholder and this will secure the netting firmly.

You could also use a single layer over the opening of the container. To do this cut a piece of 1 cm (½ in) or 2.5 cm (1 in) of chicken wire, approximately 1 cm (½ in) larger than the area you wish to cover. Place this over the opening and fold the surplus down over the edges. This method is useful for stems that need only a little support.

Other techniques

Manipulating leaves

There are many ways to manipulate leaves but the method we have used on pages 35 and 90 uses an *Aspidistra* leaf which is manipulated in the following way. Fold the tip of the *Aspidistra* down to the point where the leaf meets the stalk. Make sure the leaf is clean and dry and place a small piece of florists' fix (Plasticine® or Blutac® would also work) close to the tip. Press the two parts of the leaf together formly and you will have created a loop.

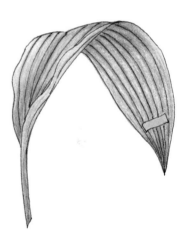

Extending stems

Bend a medium gauge stub wire so that one end is longer than the other. Place on the stem, towards the end and wrap the longer wire around the stem and the shorter end three times. The free ends should be straight and parallel to one another.

Buying summer flowers

- When purchasing sweet peas (*Lathyrus*) check that the stems are not bunched too tightly together as the bottom flowers may have been damaged. Check that none of the petals are transparent as this is a sign of age.

- Check that peonies are not too tightly closed like bullets with no colour showing. If the flower has not split it has been picked whilst immature and will not develop once cut.

- Check that sunflower (*Helianthus*) stems are strong and robust. Early in the season the stems may not be thick enough to support the heads.

- When choosing *Alstroemeria* make sure there is colour showing on at least one bud on every stem.

- *Gerbera* petals should not be too soft – place your hand gently over them to check.

- *Agapanthus* are not good early in the season – the stems need to be strong so purchase when the stems are dark and slightly speckled.

- Check that the calyx that surrounds the carnation (*Dianthus*) head is firm at the base and not split. If it is split the flower is susceptible to dehydration. Do not buy during thunderstorms as they go soft.

- Lilies are sometimes stored in a cold room for a long period so be sure they are fresh – the buds must be firm and beginning to show colour and the stems strong.

- *Celosia* and the single dark blue lisianthus (*Eustoma*) is vulnerable to botrytis – a brown mould that is unsightly and spreads rapidly – so look carefully and do not purchase if this is present.

Caring for your flowers

- When conditioning *Alstroemeria* pick off most of the lower foliage so that water goes directly to the flower and not the leaves.

- *Gerbera* are particularly susceptible to bacteria so add one drop of bleach to clean water in a clean bucket or vase.

- Remove all the foliage from larkspur and love-in-the-mist (*Nigella*) as it will become slimy in water.

- Any stem that contains a milky substance called latex (such as poppies and euphorbias) must be seared in a flame to stop the end blocking, which would prevent the uptake of water.

- Snapdragons (*Antirrhinum*) and stocks (*Matthiola*) have leaves and knobbly bits on their stems that will quickly decompose and spread bacteria if left underwater.

- Sunflowers (*Helianthus*) are happiest in shallow water.

- Dahlias are short lived and much loved by cockroaches. If purchased from a florist the insects will probably have marched elsewhere, but give them a gentle shake just in case.

- *Hydrangea* need lots of water and if purchased early in the season tend to droop. To revive the flower, first wrap the stem and head in tissue to protect it. Cut the end and place immediately in boiling water for 30 seconds. Take it out, remove the paper and place in deep water.

- It is not just the stem that takes up water, but the minute hairs on the stem itself.

- To prevent water lilies from closing, place a drop of wax into the centre of the flower.

Flower index

A selection of flowers available during the Summer months.

Blue and Purple

Agapanthus
(African lily)
white

Allium (onion)
white

Centaurea
(cornflower)
white, pink

Delphinium (larkspur)
pink, white, peach

Red and Pink

Antirrhinum
(snapdragon) yellow,
white. orange

Celosia (cockscomb)
green, orange

Chelone
white

Cirsium (thistle)
blue

Key: (F) = foliage

Gentiana (gentian)

Hydrangea
many colours

Mentha (mint)
white, pink

Scabiosa (scabious)
white, pink

Triteleia (brodiaea)

Curcuma
white

Lathyrus (sweet pea)
many colours

Paeonia (peony)
white

Phlox
white

Rosa (garden rose)
many colours

Orange and Yellow

Chrysanthemum
many colours

Eremurus (foxtail lily)
white, peach

Euphorbia
(sun spurge)
red

Helianthus
(sunflower)

White and Cream

Anthurium
(flamingo flower)
many colours

Astilbe
(false goat's beard)
pink, red

Callistephus
(China aster)
blue, pink

Chamelaucium
(wax flower)
pink, yellow

Green

Alchemilla mollis
(lady's mantle)

Amaranthus
(love-lies-bleeding)
red, pink,
ginger brown

Aspidistra
(cast iron plant)
(F)

Chrysanthemum
(bloom) many
colours

Kniphofia
(red hot poker)

Leucospermum
(pincushion protea)
red

Papaver (poppy)
red, pink, white

Sandersonia
(Chinese lantern lily)

Rosa (spray rose)
many colours

Chrysanthemum
many colours

Freesia
many colours

Hypericum
(St. John's wort)
brown, green, red,
orange, pink

Nigella
(love-in-a-mist)
blue

Triticum (wheat)

Fagus (beech)
(F)

Moluccella laevis
(bells of Ireland)

Papaver
(poppy seed head)

Chrysanthemum
(santini)
many colours

Trachelium
purple, white

Glossary

Aggregates
Coloured gravel or small stones used to add texture as well as to hide mechanics at little expense.

Aluminum wire
A very flexible wire available in a wide variety of colours and thicknesses. It is soft enough to cut with scissors.

Bullion or Boullion wire
A fine decorative wire with a curl or bend to it that gives a fine shimmer to designs.

Chicken wire
Chicken wire (sometimes known as wire netting) can be purchased from ironmongers or DIY stores in different mesh sizes and will be galvanized. If purchased from a florists' wholesalers you will have the opportunity of buying green plastic coated wire which although more expensive is gentler on the hands. Coloured decorative chicken wire is also available for contemporary work.

Decorative wire
Available in many different colours and thickness, this wire is used to add colour and create other decorative effects.

Florists' fix
An adhesive putty that is purchased on a roll. It must be used on a clean dry surface so that it will stick firmly.

Florists' tape
A strong tape that can be purchased in various widths. It is strong and waterproof.

Frog
A green plastic disc with four prongs that comes in both large and small sizes. Ideal used in conjunction with fix to secure foam.

Glass vases
The ideal size to own is 20 cm (8 in) tall. Other useful vases are a cube, two tanks – one that sits inside the other with space between, a fishbowl and a tall thin vase.

Mossing pins

Also known as German pins, these are used for securing plant material to foam. Create your own by taking a stub wire and bending it in two.

Orchid tubes

Orchids are often supplied to florists in short plastic tubes with a rubber top with a hole for the stem. Your florist may let you have these as they are often thrown away. They are also available from craft shops.

Raffia

This may be purchased in a natural tone or in a wide range of dyed colours. Raffia can be looped, made into bows or tied round containers and bunches to give a natural look.

Shells

Available in a variety of sizes, shapes and colours. You can purchase them in bags from a craft shop.

Sisal

Sisal is a natural material derived from *Agave sisalana* leaves. It is available in a wide range of colours and is very useful filler.

Spray mount

Spray mount or spray glue allows you to reposition items as often as you wish. Sprayed lightly it will not seep through and damage fabric.

Stem tape

This is used to disguise wires that have been added to extend or give support to fresh plant material. It also slows down the evaporation of water from the stem.

Stub wires

Lengths of wire (as opposed to wire on a reel) used in floristry for extending, supporting or replacing stems. Wires are measured by gauge. The wire used must be the lightest possible needed to support the head of the flower you are wiring.

NB

Many of the items mentioned in the Glossary can be purchased from Hobbycraft in the UK (www.hobbycraft.co.uk) and from Michaels in the USA (www.michaels.com) or from craft shops and garden centres.

The Judith Blacklock Flower School

The Judith Blacklock Flower School offers intensive, structured courses in all aspects of flower arranging and the business of floristry. In a quiet secluded mews in Knightsbridge, London, Judith and her team of dedicated teachers give professional information and practical learning skills, using the most beautiful flowers and foliage, that are relevant to participants from all over the world.

From basic design through to the most advanced contemporary work there is a course suitable for every level of expertise.

Private, team building and structured group lessons are available on request.

The Judith Blacklock Flower School
4/5 Kinnerton Place South, London SW1X 8EH
Tel. +44 (0)20 7235 6235
school@judithblacklock.com
www.judithblacklock.com

Acknowledgements

Photography

Judith Blacklock: pages 3, 12, 13, 21, 24, 25, 35, 36, 37, 40, 41, 60, 61, 63, 66, 67, 71, 83, 87, 89
Oliver Gordon: pages 30, 45
Lyndon Parker: pages 3, 17, 59
Tobias Smith: pages 5, 6, 7, 9, 10, 11, 15, 18, 19, 22, 23, 26, 27, 28, 29, 31, 32, 33, 35, 38, 39, 43, 47, 48, 49, 50, 51, 52, 53, 55, 57, 65, 68, 69, 72, 73, 76, 77, 79, 80, 81, 85, 91
Steve Tanner: page 75

© iStockphoto.com/Richard Viard: pages 1, 99
© iStockphoto.com/Sandra Ford: page 2
© iStockphoto.com/Hon Fai Ng: page 101
© iStockphoto.com/Zina Seletskaya: page 106

Line Drawings: Tomoko Nakamoto
Botanical Editor: Dr. Christina Curtis
Assistant Editor: Rachel Petty

Thanks to David Austin Roses for their wonderful fragrant roses featured on pages 14–15 that are always a joy to use.

As with all my recipe books I have received enormous help and inspiration from the people with whom I work and my students from all over the world. Rachel Petty has been a great help in putting the book together. Wendy Andrade and Dawn Jennings – amazing teachers at my school – have given most valuable advice and assistance.

My mother Joan Ward has let me have the run of her house and flower arranging cupboard to come up with photos in the magnificent setting of Cumbria. She is the one who led me into the world of flowers.

Amanda Hawkes continues with her flawless work and magic to create a book with which I am proud to be associated. My thanks to her.

Once more I thank Christina Curtis and Tomoko Nakamoto for their kind and most valued input into this book of summer flower recipes.